Addai and Mari
—the Anaphora
of the Apostles:
A Text for Students

with Introduction, Translation, and Commentary

by

Bryan D. Spinks

Churchill College, Cambridge

GROVE BOOKS

BRAMCOTE NOTTS.

CONTENTS

PREFACE

For many years F. E. Brightman's *Liturgies Eastern and Western* provided a useful English translation of the anaphora of the Apostles Addai and Mari. The publication of the Mar Esa'ya text of the anaphora in 1966, and the critical edition of the anaphora called *Sharar* in 1973, and the host of subsequent studies have rendered Brightman's text obsolete as a primary text. Although a few English translations of the Mar Esa'ya text have been published, in the main these have been from the Latin translation, and carry the defects of a translation of a translation.

This edition seeks to provide the student with a translation from the Syriac, together with the text of *Sharar*, as far as possible bringing out the similarities between the two anaphoras.

I would like to express my thanks to Professor Sebastian Brock who kindly offered advice when I first made a translation of *Sharar* some years ago, and for so readily answering questions which arose from the present work.

I am pleased also to record my great debt to the Reverend Douglas Webb of Wilburton, Ely, who not only offered suggestions for a smoother and more literal translation, but who has also generously checked and supplemented the variant readings given in W. F. Macomber's Syriac edition of 1966. His kindness has made the text a useful tool for the more advanced student.

The front cover includes a pastiche of printed texts in different languages and editions.

Bryan D. Spinks
October 1980

ABBREVIATIONS

ATR	*Anglican Theological Review*
JTS	*Journal of Theological Studies*
EL	*Ephemerides Liturgicae*
OC	*Oriens Christianus*
OCA	*Orientalia Christiana Analecta*
OCP	*Orientalia Christiana Periodica*
SP	*Studia Patristica*
TS	*Theological Studies*

First Impression December 1980

ISSN 0306 0608
ISBN 0 905422 93 7

INTRODUCTION

The East Syrian Liturgical Tradition

For many years now the area of East Syria has been regarded as important for liturgical research, both on account of its Semitic background, and its later isolation from the rest of Christendom. A considerable number of recent studies have drawn attention to the Judaeo-Christian origin of Syriac-speaking Christianity which centred upon Edessa and Nisibis, and to the strong Jewish influence which was exerted from the region of Adiabene.[1] The *Peshitta,* the Syriac Old Testament, appears to have been a Jewish production, in fact another Targum; and the great Syrian theologians, Aphrahat and Ephraem, seem to have been considerably influenced by Jewish sectarian teaching.[2] Robert Murray suggests that, although the Syriac Church was definitely separated from Judaism by the fourth century, in certain important respects it still remained spiritually close to the parent Synagogue.[3] Furthermore, this area had a long history of resisting repeated attempts to Hellenize it, and was strongly anti-Byzantine in spirit. After the Council of Ephesus in 431, many of the bishops of this area rejected the Christology of Cyril of Alexandria in favour of that of the deposed teacher, Nestorius, and as the Nestorian Church it was later re-organized with its centre at Nisibis in the Persian Empire, and was effectively insulated linguistically, culturally, and politically, from the rest of Christendom.[4] Not unnaturally, therefore, liturgical scholars have paid particular attention to the liturgical tradition of the Edessene Church.

The East Syrian Eucharistic tradition is represented by the anaphoras of the *Apostles Addai and Mari* (**AM**), *Theodore of Mopsuestia,* and *Nestorius.* A fragment published by R. H. Connolly seems to belong to this tradition[5], but others, if they actually existed, have since disappeared.[6] The anaphoras attributed to *Theodore* and *Nestorius* were certainly originally composed in Greek, and subsequently translated into Syriac. They show clear signs of West Syrian influence, and have received relatively little attention from liturgical scholars.[7] However, quite the reverse is true of **AM,** which is an original Syriac composition. Although the late Bayard H. Jones believed that it represents a prècis of *Nestorius,* dating from the early seventh century[8], most scholars, taking its semitic character more seriously, have

[1] For the literature see Robert Murray *Symbols of Church and Kingdom. A Study in Early Syriac Tradition* (CUP, 1975).

[2] *Ibid.*

[3] *Ibid.,* p.18.

[4] See G. Dix *The Shape of the Liturgy* (Dacre/Black, London, 1945) pp.173-178.

[5] R. H. Connolly, 'Sixth-Century Fragments of an East-Syrian Anaphora' in *Oriens Christianus* NS 12-14 (1925), pp.99-128.

[6] F. E. Brightman and C. E. Hammond *Liturgies Eastern and Western* Vol. 1. *Eastern Liturgies* (OUP, 1896) p.lxxx.

[7] F. E. Brightman, 'The Anaphora of Theodore', in *JTS* 31 (1930) pp.160-164; Bayard H. Jones, 'The Sources of the Nestorian Liturgy' in *ATR* 46 (1964) pp.414-425; 'The Formation of the Nestorian Liturgy' in *ATR* 48 (1966) pp.276-306; L. Bouyer *Eucharist* tr. C. U. Quinn (Notre Dame, Indiana, 1968) pp.342ff; B. Botte, 'Les Anaphores Syriennes Orientales' in *Eucharisties d'Orient et d'Occident* 2 (Les Editions du Cerf, Paris, 1970). W. F. Macomber is in the process of preparing critical texts of these two anaphoras.

[8] Bayard H. Jones, 'The History of the Nestorian Liturgies' in *ATR* 46 (1964) pp.157-176, esp. p.174.

dated it variously between the second and fourth centuries, and regard it as an important witness in understanding the growth and development of the early eucharistic prayer.[1]

The Earliest Text of AM

AM is known in three textual traditions:

(1) The Nestorian.
(2) The Chaldean Church, having its centre at Mosul, being that part of the Nestorian Church which became a uniat Church in communion with Rome in the seventeenth century.
(3) The Malabar Church in India, also a uniat Church.

Prior to 1966 it seemed that only six manuscripts—two from around 1500, and four others of the sixteenth century—were available for establishing a critical text of this anaphora. That the list given by Brightman[2] was woefully inadequate was being established by the patient work of Douglas Webb of Wilburton, Ely, and by William F. Macomber in the U.S.A.[3] In 1966 Macomber published a list of earlier manuscripts, together with a critical edition of **AM**, based on the text from a *Hudra* (the book containing the proper of the liturgy and of the offices for Sundays, feasts of our Lord, and the principal saints' days) belonging to the Church of Mar Esa'ya in Mosul, which he dated as tenth/eleventh century.[4] So far this dating has not been challenged, and its text of **AM** has been regarded as the earliest form of the anaphora that we at present have. The structure of the anaphoras as given in Brightman and in the Mar Esa'ya text can be summarized as follows:

[CUSHAPA—a private prayer of the celebrant said kneeling and in a low voice.
GEHANTA—an inclination—a prayer said in a low voice and with inclined head.
QANONA—an audible conclusion to a GEHANTA]

BRIGHTMAN (pp.283-288)	*MAR ESA'YA*
A DIALOGUE	*A* DIALOGUE
CUSHAPA	
B GEHANTA—Praise and Thanks-giving.	*B* GEHANTA—Praise and Thanks-giving.
C QANONA —Sanctus with its in-troduction.	*C* QANONA —Sanctus with its in-troduction.
CUSHAPA	
D GEHANTA—Thanksgiving for re-demption.	*D* GEHANTA—Thanksgiving for re-demption.
QANONA—Doxology.	QANONA—Doxology.
CUSHAPA	
E GEHANTA—Commemoration of the righteous fathers. Petition for peace.	*E* GEHANTA—Commemoration of the righteous fathers. Petition for peace.

[1] E.g. B. Bott, 'L'Anaphore Chaldéene des Apôtres' in *Orientalia Christiana Periodica* 15 (1949) pp.259-276.

[2] Brightman *Liturgies Eastern and Western*, p.lxxix.

[3] For their respective results, D. Webb, 'Variations dans les versions manuscrites de la liturgie nestorienne d'Addai et de Mari' in *Sacris Erudiri* 18 (1967-68) pp.478-523; W. F. Macomber, 'The oldest known text of the Anaphora of the Apostles Addai and Mari' in *OCP* 31 (1966) pp.335-371.

[4] W. F. Macomber *art. cit.*

F	Petition for all the Church.	F	Petition for all the Church.
G	Commemoration of the mystery of Christ.	G	Commemoration of the mystery of Christ.
H	Epiklesis	H	Epiklesis
I	QANONA—Doxology	I	QANONA—Doxology

Although there are some important verbal differences, the major difference is that the Mar Esa'ya text lacks the *cushapa* intercessions.

Some Textual Problems of AM

By far the most puzzling textual problem of **AM** is the apparent absence of any institution narrative. The East Syrian manuscripts, including Mar Esa'ya, lack an institution narrative. In the Urmiah missal of the Archbishop of Canterbury's mission, 1890, printed for the Nestorians, the editors inserted 1 Cor. 11.23-25 at a point which seemed suitable, namely before the *cushapa* 'O Lord of Hosts, accept this offering', and the *gehanta* commemorating the righteous fathers (*E*). Similarly, in the Catholic Chaldean Missal (Mosul 1901 and 1936) an institution narrative has been inserted in the middle of the post-sanctus prayer (*D*). In neither instance is there any manuscript authority for such insertions.

This apparent omission in the manuscripts finds confirmation in the Malabar liturgy. By means of a detailed concordance R. H. Connolly and Edmund Bishop illustrated that the Malabar liturgy was essentially the same liturgy as **AM**; they were in fact one and the same liturgy.[1] The present Malabar use which goes back to the printed missal of 1774 (Rozian), and the version of the rite published by Antonio de Gouvea in 1606 (Menezian)[2], both contain an institution narrative, but after the anaphora and before the fraction (the two versions differ over the precise location). An earlier Malabrese manuscript, *Vat. Syr. 66,* attributed to Mar Joseph Sulaqa, Metropolitan of India 1556-1569, contains a narrative before the liturgy which the author intended to be recited at the end of the ceremonies of the fraction. Thus the rite of Malabar witnesses to the fact that on its arrival in India, the anaphora of **AM** contained no institution narrative. Did it ever contain such a narrative, and if it did, when and why was it removed?

Another problem is raised by the fact that part of **AM** is addressed to the Father, and part to the Son. Was the author a muddle-headed monarchian, or does it represent later re-writing? Paragraph *G*, which commemorated the mystery of Christ, has no main verb, and it is not clear as to the identity and function of this prayer. A number of studies have questioned the antiquity of the intercessions, the sanctus, and the epiklesis (*C, E, F, H*). These problems have resulted in repeated attempts to reconstruct a 'primitive' text of **AM**.

Textual Reconstruction before the Mar Esa'ya Text

(1)   In the very influential article published in 1929, E. C. Ratcliff attempted to reconstruct the eucharistic prayer of the old Edessene Church

[1] R. H. Connolly, E. Bishop, 'The Work of Menezes on the Malabar Liturgy' in *JTS* 15 (1914) pp.396-425, 569-589; F. C. Burkitt, 'The Old Malabar Liturgy 'in *JTS* 29 (1928) pp.155-157.

[2] Placid of S. Joseph, 'The Present Syro-Malabar Liturgy: Menezian or Rozian?' in *OCP* 23 (1957) pp.313-331.

which he believed was embedded in **AM**.[1] Accepting that **AM** had never contained an institution narrative, he questioned much of the remainder of the prayer in the manuscript tradition represented by the version of Brightman. Arguing from the outline given in Narsai's liturgical homilies, and following up a suggestion of Edmund Bishop, Ratcliff excised both the *cushapa* and *gehanta* intercessions.[2] Of the remaining text, he believed the sanctus and epiklesis to be later interpolations, in both cases because the clauses introducing them appeared to have no connection with what preceded them, though he allowed that the epiklesis may have once occupied a position outside the anaphora.[3] The doxology after the second *gehanta* which divided the anaphora in two he suggested was a doublet introduced on account of the intruding intercessions. Furthermore, in paragraph *G,* he suggested that the words 'great and fearful and holy and life-giving and divine' should be omitted as destroying the balance of the antithesis between 'example' and 'likeness' (Brightman=mystery). With the removal of the redundant post-sanctus phrase 'with these heavenly hosts', Ratcliff recast the pattern of **AM** as a single prayer of three paragraphs: an address of praise to the name of the creator and redeemer; a thanksgiving for what he has done for men; a solemn following of Christ's example and a special commemoration of his redemptive death and resurrection, for which again praise and thanks are offered to the divine name. He suggested that the prayer, originally addressed to Christ, was essentially a hymn of thanksgiving, and labelled it a 'Eucharistia', a rite which came somewhere in between the Mass and the Agape.

(2) In *The Shape of the Liturgy* Gregory Dix accepted much of Ratcliff's suggested reconstruction: the prayer was originally addressed to Christ; the preface and sanctus, the intercessions and first doxology were interpolations. However, on two important points Dix differed from Ratcliff. In paragraph *G,* where the grammar is difficult because there is no main verb, and the address changes from the Son to 'the Father, he suggested the words 'rejoicing, glorifying . . . Christ' were a later interpolation. Dix also defended the authenticity of the Epiklesis, arguing that Holy Spirit here was to be equated with the *shekinah* rather than the third person of the Trinity.[4]

(3) In an article published in 1949, and later modified and elaborated in 1965[5], Bernard Botte analyzed **AM**. He argued that its style,

[1] E. C. Ratcliff, 'The Original Form of the Anaphora of Addai and Mari: A Suggestion' in *JTS* 30 (1928-29) pp.23-32.

[2] *Ibid.,* p.27.

[3] In fact, at a later date, Ratcliff's private opinion was that the original form of **AM** had concluded with the sanctus. See my essay, 'The Cleansed Leper's Thankoffering before the Lord: Edward Craddock Ratcliff and the Pattern of the Early Anaphora', forthcoming in ed. Bryan D. Spinks *The Sacrifice of Praise* (Centro Liturgico Vincenziano—Edizioni Liturgiche, Rome, 1980).

[4] G. Dix *The Shape of the Liturgy* p.184.

[5] B. Botte, 'L'Anaphore Chaldéene des Apôtres' in *OCP* 15 (1949) pp.259-276; 'Problemes de l'Anaphore syrienne des Apôtres Addai et Mari' in *L'Orient Syrien* 10 (1965) pp.89-106.

characterized by a constant parallelism, betrays its Semitic origin, and its early date. He accepted Ratcliff's arguments concerning the sanctus and the introductory words of paragraph *D,* and likewise his views on the intercessions and epiklesis—though the latter showed clear signs of being a Semitic composition, and not a copy from Greek sources. He did not accept that the anaphora was originally addressed to the Son, but rather that the oscillation between Father and Son reflects unconscious monarchianism. However, Botte found it strange that an anaphora should contain neither an institution narrative nor an epiklesis. He noted the difficulty in translating paragraph *G,* where, with one exception, the verbs are participles with the prenominal suffix. Brightman had translated it thus:

'And we also, O my Lord, thy weak and frail and miserable servants who are gathered together in thy name, both stand before thee at this time and have received the example which is from thee delivered unto us, rejoicing and praising and exalting and commemorating and celebrating this great and fearful and holy and lifegiving and divine mystery of the passion and the death and the burial and the resurrection of our Lord and our Saviour Jesus Christ.

Botte, however, gave a slightly different rendering:

'And we also, O Lord, thy weak and frail and miserable servants who are gathered together in thy name and stand before thee at this time, we also have received by tradition the Type [Latin. French 'l'example'] which is from thee, rejoicing, [etc.]'[1]

Botte found a hiatus at the beginning of this paragraph, and the words seemed to him to require a foregoing sentence. Furthermore, the last part of the paragraph, 'commemorating . . . resurrection' recalls the phraseology found in the classical anamnesis which follows an institution narrative. In *Theodore* an anamnesis is found which has similar wording to the paragraph of **AM**, but there it follows an institution narrative which has a peculiar form:

'And with his holy Apostles in that night in which he was betrayed, he celebrated this great and holy and divine mystery, taking the bread in his holy hands. And he blessed and brake, and gave it to his disciples, and said, This is my body which is broken for the life of the world for the remission of sins. After the same manner also he gave thanks over the cup, and gave to them, and said, This is my blood of the New Testament which is shed for many for the remission of sins. Take all of you therefore. Eat of this bread and drink of this cup. Do this whensoever you come together for my memorial.

And as we have been commanded, so we your lowly, weak and miserable servants have come together, that by permission of your grace we may celebrate this great and awful and holy and divine mystery, wherein great salvation was wrought for the whole human race.' (from the Urmiah edition)

[1] The English translation here tries to do justice to Botte's Latin (1949) and French (1965) translations, and his discussion of terminology (1949, pp.267-8).

Botte also noted references to the institution narrative in Ephraem and Aphrahat where the ending was 'whenever you are gathered together in my name'. Paragraph G of **AM** would seem to follow on from a particular Syriac form of narrative, and Botte identified it as an anamnesis. The conclusion he drew from this is that the anamnesis is the record of an institution narrative that has since disappeared. He suggested three phases of development:

(a) Thanksgiving and recital of institution with anamnesis.
(b) Thanksgiving with shortened recital of institution and epiklesis.
(c) Thanksgiving and epiklesis without recital of institution.

In his article of 1965, Botte suggested a reordering of the text of **AM** to bring it in line with those of *Theodore* and *Nestorius*—thanksgiving, institution, anamnesis, intercessions, epiklesis.

Most of Botte's recommendations have been endorsed by Louis Bouyer, who provides a reconstructed text with institution narrative according to the former's suggestions of 1965.[1]

(4) Whereas most scholars have regarded the intercessions of **AM** as later interpolations, more caution was shown by H. Engberding[2], who compared them with the intercessions of the other two East Syrian anaphoras, and an anaphora of the Maronite Church (the Syrian Church which is mainly located in Lebanon and Israel, and which since the time of the crusades has been a uniat Church), called *The Anaphora of St. Peter III,* or *Sharar.*[3] He concluded that the intercessions constitute part of the earliest form of the prayer, and that a doublet of petitions resulted from a borrowing of the intercessions of *Theodore.* Furthermore, Engberding disputed the identification of paragraph G as an anamnesis. He found similar constructions spread widely in the intercessions where, after a prayer for the dead, there occurs one for the living introduced by 'We also'. A very similar paragraph is found in *Nestorius.* According to Engberding, paragraph G is a continuation of the prayer for the living and forms part of the intercessions. It is not an anamnesis, and therefore there is no place which invites an institution narrative; **AM**'s original structure was praise and petition.

(5) In a paper which was published posthumously, Bayard H. Jones[4] examined the history of the references to **AM** in Syrian literature, and the history of its title, and argued that it was a prècis of *Nestorius* resulting from the reforms which are alleged to have been made by Iso'yab III (649-659) in the seventh century. The 'primitive' form of **AM** is *Nestorius*.

The Mar Esa'ya Text of AM

Concluding his article of 1965, Botte wrote, 'short of a sensational discovery, we will always be in doubt'.[5] The following year W. F. Macomber

[1] L. Bouyer *Eucharist* pp.147-158.
[2] H. Engberding, 'Zum anaphorischen Furbittgebet der Ostsyrischen Liturgie der Apostel Addaj und Mar (j)' *Oriens Christianus* 41 (1957) pp.102-124.
[3] *Sharar,* meaning 'confirm' or 'strengthen', is a title given to this anaphora, it being the opening word of a prayer of the pre-anaphora.
[4] See note 1 on p.4 above.
[5] *Art. cit.,* p.106.

published what has come to be regarded as 'a sensational discovery', namely, the text of **AM** in a *hudra* of the Church of Mar Esa'ya, which on paleographical grounds he dated to the tenth or eleventh century—five centuries earlier than the text used by Ratcliff and Botte.[1] The broad characteristics of this text are as follows:

(a) The anaphora lacks the *cushapa* intercessions. Although one of the features of the *hudra* is abbreviation, and although another early manuscript discovered by Macomber, the twelfth century Diarbekir *hudra,* does contain them, Macomber concluded that these intercessions were not generally introduced into the East Syrian liturgy before the end of the thirteenth century, and that Ratcliff's suggestions on this matter were correct.

(b) The sanctus is contained in the Mar Esa'ya text, but Macomber accepted Ratcliff's opinion that it was a later addition to the anaphora.

(c) There is no institution narrative—Macomber suggested that it was removed by a reform carried out by Iso'yab III.

(d) The phrase 'in your name' upon which Botte built much of his argument for an institution narrative, is absent; also, the word 'and' introducing the epiklesis is absent, a point which Ratcliff regarded as supporting his view that this section was not original to the anaphora.[2]

No one has challenged Macomber's dating of the Mar Esa'ya text, and liturgical scholars seem to have accepted without question that its readings are to be preferred to those of other manuscripts.

Maronite Sharar

The close relationship that exists between **AM** and the Maronite anaphora called *Sharar* was pointed out long ago by I. E. Rahmani and A. Baumstark, and had been investigated by Engberding.[3] Most of **AM** is contained in *Sharar,* and the relationship points to a common origin, or a common source underlying both anaphoras.

In publishing the Mar Esa'ya text, Macomber provided the first critical text of **AM**, and included readings of *Sharar* amongst the variant readings. In a later article, Macomber made a comparison between **AM** and *Sharar* with regard to three points.[4]

(a) The Prefatory dialogue. According to Macomber, **AM** has been influenced by and expanded from *Theodore.* The East Syrian blessing of the oil of baptism seems to preserve an earlier form. By comparing it with the dialogue of *Sharar,* Macomber offered a reconstruction of the common source used by the two anaphoras.

---

[1] The precise dating is difficult since there is no reproduction available of a dated sample of the so-called 'Nestorian' cursive writing earlier than 1243 A.D. While some parts of the manuscript are thirteenth century additions, the original part is older, and a marginal note is written in a hand which resembles two lines of British Museum Additional Manuscript 17.923, dated 1074 A.D.

[2] See my essay in *The Sacrifice of Praise.*

[3] I. E. Rahmani *Testamentum Domini Nostri Jesu Christi* (Mosul 1899); A. Baumstark, 'Altlibanesishe Liturgie' in *Oriens Christianus* 4 (1904), pp.190-194; H. Engberding' 'Urgestalt, Eingenart und Entwicklung eines altantiochenischen eucharistischen Hochgebetes' in *Oriens Christianus* 29 (1932) pp.32-48.

[4] W. F. Macomber, 'The Maronite and Chaldean Versions of the Anaphora of the Apostles' in *OCP* 37 (1971) pp.55-84.

(b) Since the whole of *Sharar* from the post-sanctus to the final doxology is addressed to the Son, Macomber accepted Ratcliff's opinion that **AM** too was originally addressed to the Son. The Pre-sanctus has been adapted to praise the Trinity.

(c) The Maronite anaphora contains an institution narrative, having a peculiar form, addressed to the Son, and embedded in intercessions in a block coming between paragraphs corresponding to *E* and *F* of **AM**. Macomber suggested that the Maronite anaphora has preserved both the location and form of the institution narrative now absent from **AM**.

The common source, he has argued further, was an anaphora of the Aramaic-speaking Church which had its centre at Edessa. After the schism of the fifth century, it was preserved in the East Syrian Church, and the Aramaic-speaking areas of Lebanon and the Orontes valley.[1]

Textual Reconstruction of the Anaphora of the Apostles

For his comparison of the two anaphoras, Macomber had had to use the text of *Sharar* in a Maronite missal of 1594, as no critical edition existed. This gap was filled in 1973 when J. M. Sauget published a critical text in the series *Anaphorae Syriacae*.[2] With good texts of both anaphoras available, recent studies have been concerned with reconstructing the common source, the anaphora of the apostles, rather than simply proposing emendations to **AM**. To date these studies have fallen into two groups.

(1) In their general studies of the origin of the eucharistic prayer, Louis Ligier, Louis Bouyer, and Thomas Talley[3], have regarded the three *gehantas* of **AM** as corresponding to the three *berakoth* of *Didache* 10, and behind them both, the three berakoth of the Jewish meal prayer, the *Birkat ha-mazon*. Accepting this correspondence, and building on the suggestions of Macomber, reconstructions have been offered by Jose Manuel Sanchez Caro[4] and H. A. J. Wegman.[5]

Sanchez Caro reconstructs the text as follows:

Paragraph *B*, without any reference to Father, Son and Spirit.
D.
E, excluding 'who have been pleasing in your sight', 'your Messiah' and the petition for peace.
adding   'as you have taught us *through your holy gospel'*.
Institution narrative, from *Sharar*.
Anamnesis, based on *Sharar* and *G*.
F, reconstructed.
I,

1 W. F. Macomber, 'A Theory on the origins of the Syrian, Maronite and Chaldean Rites' in *OCP* 39 (1973) pp.235-242.

2 *Anaphorae Syriacae.* Vol. II Fasc. 3 (Pontificium Institutum Orientalium Studiorum, Rome, 1973) pp.275-323.

3 L. Ligier, 'The origins of the Eucharistic Prayer: From the Last Supper to the Eucharist' in *Studia Liturgica* 9 (1973) pp.161-185; L. Bouyer *Eucharist*, pp.154-155; T. J. Talley, 'The Eucharistic Prayer of the Ancient Church According to Recent Research: Results and Reflections 'in *Studia Liturgica* 11 (1976), pp.138-158.

4 J. M. Sanchez Caro, 'La anafora de Addai y Mari y la anafora meronita sarrar: intento de reconstruccion de la fuente primitiva comun' in *OCP* 43 (1977) pp.41-69.

5 H. A. J. Wegman, 'Pleidooi voor een Teskst de Anaphora van de Apostelen Addai en Mari' in *Bijdragen* 40 (1979) pp.15-43.

The reconstructed prayer begins by addressing God in the second person, and then switches to the third person, which is explained as following the pattern of Jewish *berakoth*. Sanchez Caro suggests that later evolution of the text saw the introduction of the sanctus, borrowed from the *Qedussah de Yoser* of the Synagogue morning service, and an epiklesis; later still, reference to the Trinity was introduced into *B*. After the fifth century schisms, the anaphora developed differently in the two Churches, and the East Syrian version lost its institution narrative probably in the liturgical reform of Iso'yab III.

Herman Wegman has also offered a reconstruction of the 'primitive' form of the prayer. In his opinion, the prayer was a table prayer in four strophes, comparable to the *Didache* 10 and the *Birkat ha-mazon,* the fourth strophe being a kind of *chatimah,* or concluding doxology. The prayer consisted of paragraphs: *B,* without reference to the Trinity.

$$D$$
$$E$$
$$I$$

A second stage of development saw the introduction of an institution narrative (preserved in *Sharar*), with anamnesis and epiklesis (*G* and *H*). In his opinion, *F* represents an even later addition.

W. F. Macomber has also, at the time of writing, prepared a reconstruction of the common form, c.400 A.D., which makes use of a considerable amount of material found only in *Sharar*.[1]

(2) While many scholars have seen a tripartite structure in **AM,** Jacob Vellian has drawn attention to the similarities in structure and theme which exist between **AM** and the Synagogue morning berakoth before the *Shema,* the *Yoser* and the *Ahabah*.[2] *Yoser* gives praise for creation and ends with the *Qedussah* (Isaiah 6.3); the *Ahabah* is a recalling of the gifts of God's love, such as the Torah and the land; it includes a commemoration of the fathers, and has a petition for peace. The doxologies of **AM** divide the anaphora in two; the first part, *A-D,* has a similar focus to *Yoser* with *Qedussah,* adding a general commemoration of the economy of Christ. There are also similarities between the themes of *E, F* and *I,* and of the *Ahabah*. Vellian writes:

> 'If we follow the pattern of the morning *berakoth* in question, we may not find any place which explicitly invites the Institution-Narrative. So it could be that the Anaphora of Addai and Mari, which does not give any glimpse of the Institution-Narrative prior to the sixteenth century, was composed after the pattern of the morning *berakoth*.'[3]

---

[1] 'The Ancient Form of the Anaphora of the Apostles' to appear as a Dumbarton Oaks Paper. I am grateful to Dr. Macomber for allowing me to see his proposed reconstruction before its publication.

[2] J. Vellian, 'The Anaphoral Structure of Addai and Mari compared to the Berakoth Preceding the Shema in the Synagogue Morning Service contained in Seder R. Amram Gaon' in *Le Muséon* 85 (1972) pp.201-223.

[3] *Ibid.* p.217.

The present writer has, with considerable qualifications, supported Vellian's approach.[1] Vellian used the Synagogue prayers as found in the eighth century A.D. Seder *Amran Gaon,* which are too late for a useful comparison. However, the comparison is still valid when made with earlier forms of the Synagogue *berakoth.* **AM** may represent an anaphora with a bipartite structure, *A-D* and *E-I,* and a second century date would not be impossible. Comparing **AM** with the Maronite anaphora, it is evident that the Maronite version often preserves a better reading, and must be taken seriously in reconstructing the common source. Every paragraph of **AM** has a parallel in *Sharar,* with the exception of *G.* It would seem logical that the parallel material represents the common source, and all other material probably represents independent additions and development. On this basis *G* is an addition to **AM,** but also the institution narrative of *Sharar,* and its anamnesis, must be regarded as an addition. *G* may well be an anamnesis marking the place of an institution narrative, added by the East Syrian redactor; the Maronite redactor chose a different position for his institution narrative, and provided a very different anamnesis.

An Original Form?

The publication of the Mar Esa'ya text of **AM** and of a critical text of *Sharar* has encouraged renewed speculation on the anaphora of the apostles, and the quest for its 'original text'. At present there is no consensus regarding solutions to all the problems which the texts present. As Emmanuel Cutrone puts it, 'it is only painfully obvious that there is still mystery and enigma associated with Addai and Mari'.[2] However, it is possible that attempts to reconstruct a single 'original text' are misleading, and that we can do no more than identify the common material found in the two anaphoras. Writing on the Jewish *berakoth,* Joseph Heinemann emphasized:

'We must not try to determine by philosophical methods the "original" text of any prayer without first determining whether or not such an "original" text ever existed. For we are dealing with materials which originated as part of an oral tradition and hence by their very nature were not phrased in any fixed uniform formulation—which at a later stage came to be "revised" and expanded—but rather were improvised on the spot; and, subsequently, "re-improvised" and reworded in many different formulations in an equally spontaneous fashion.'[3]

Early eucharistic prayers may have followed some outline, but they were the free composition of the bishop, or president.[4] If the Anaphora of the Apostles is early, and if we are to take its Semitic background seriously, it may be that we have two developed, or 're-improvised' and reworded, versions of a once oral tradition. It is perhaps more accurate to speak of a common tradition rather than of an 'original text'.

1 Bryan D. Spinks 'The Original Form of the Anaphora of the Apostles: A Suggestion in the Light of Maronite Sharar' in *Ephemerides Liturgicae* 91 (1977) pp.146-161.

2 E. Cutrone 'The Anaphora of the Apostles: Implications of the Mar Esa'ya Text' in *Theological Studies* 43 (1973) pp.624-642.

3 J. Heinemann *Prayer in the Talmud. Forms and Patterns* (Walter De Gruyter, Berlin and New York, 1977) p.42.

4 R. P. C. Hanson, 'The Liberty of the Bishop to improvise Prayer in the Eucharist' in *Vigiliae Christianae* 15 (1961) pp.173-175.

THE TEXT

On the left hand side is given a translation of **AM** from the Mar Esa'ya text published by Macomber, from the opening dialogue to the conclusion. The division into paragraphs is to facilitate following the various studies referred to in the Introduction. On the right hand side is given a translation of *Sharar* from the text published by Sauget. Both translations have been made from the Syriac, and are as literal as possible. As far as possible, the translation of words has been consistent in order that the texts may be accurately compared. In the text of *Sharar,* the following representation has been used to illustrate the common material: Continuous underlining represents continuous common words; discontinuous underlining represents common words, but a broken sequence or different word order; broken underlining represents that the word has a common Syriac root; double underlining represents material in *Sharar* found in other manuscripts of **AM;** the underlining with dots draws attention to a phrase which is repeated in *Sharar;* and finally, asterisks mark two words whose roots are used elsewhere in **AM,** but are not utilized by *Sharar* in its corresponding paragraph.

For the more advanced reader, the variant readings of **AM** are given, according to Macomber's list, as follows:

A—Diarbekir hudra	..	12th	a—Khoshaba ritual	.. ..	1664
B—Mardin 22	..	1287	b—Ming. Syr. 53	..	1681
C—Cambr. Add. 2046B	..	15th	c—Diarbekir ritual	.. ..	1683
D—Diarbekir 48 ..	..	15th	d—Mosul 41	..	1685
E—Mardin 19 ..	..	15th	e—Cambr. Add. 2045	..	1686
F—Chald. Patr. 333	..	15th	f—Vat. Syr. 491	..	1686
G—Br. Mus. Or. 5750	.. ..	15th	g—Cambr. Oo.1.15	..	1691
H—Berlin 38	..	1496	h—Vat. Syr. 44	..	1691
I—Chald. Patr. 36	..	15/16th	i—Chald. Patr. 38	..	1697
J—Berlin 39	..	17th	j—Berlin 40	..	17/18th
K—Rouen Or. 21	..	16th	k—Vat. Borg. Syr. 36	..	17/18th
L—Saigh hudra	..	16th	l—Vat. Syr. 43	..	1701
M—Br. Mus. Or. 4060 ..	..	16th	m—Chald. Patr. 170	..	1706
N—Vat. Borg. Syr. 150	..	16th	n—Chald. Patr. 39	..	1708
O—Vat. Syr. 66	..	16th	o—Mardin ritual	..	1715
P—Alqosh 70	..	1564	p—Chald. Patr. 37	..	1726
Q—Mardin 20 ..	..	1566	q—Mardin ritual	..	18th
R—Br. Mus.Add. 7181	..	1570	r—Mardin ritual	..	18th
S—N-D. des Sem. 92	..	1578	s—Mardin 31 ..	..	1753
T—Mardin ritual	..	1584/5	t—Berlin 42	..	1756
U—Chald. Patr. 40	..	1600	u—Cambr. Add. 2046A		18/19th
V—Chald. Patr. 209	..	16/17th	v—Chald. Patr. 42	..	1809
W—Vat. Syr. 42	..	1603	w—Berlin 41 ..	..	1834
X—Mardin 18 ..	..	1605	x—Chald. Patr. 221	..	1839
Y—Vat. Syr. 303	..	1608	y—Mar Ya'qob 6	..	1850
Z—Ming. Syr. 611	..	17th	z—McHardy codex	..	1908

AQ Alqosh tradition, R.S.U.Y.b.c.d.e.i.j.n.p.s.t.u.v.
CH Chaldean tradition, f.g.h.l.m.o.q.r.x.y.
ML Malabar tradition, Z.k.
Cm Mosul editions of the Chaldean missal, 1901 and 1936.
Cr Roman edition of the Chaldean missal.
Ke Nestorian edition of Kelaita, where it differs from the Anglican.
Mb Editions of the Malabar missal, 1929 and 1960.

[continued at top of both pages 14 and 15]

Mn	Latin translations of Malabar Liturgy as corrected by de Menezes.
Re	Latin translation of Renaudot.
Sr	*Sharar*
Tr	Textus receptus (=*Ke* and *Ur*, where they agree)
Ur	Anglican edition of Urmiah.
Edd	All of the printed editions (not translations) where they agree.

TEXT—AM

[N.B. All the apparatus notes which follow—whether on left hand or right hand pages—
—relate to the **AM** text on the left hand page. The numbers in the notes refer to the line
in the section of text.]

A

And the priest says:	Peace be with you.
And they reply:	And with you and your spirit.
And the deacon says:	Give peace to one another in the love of Christ.
And they say:	For all the Catholikoi.
And the deacon proclaims:	Let us give thanks and intercede.
And the priest says:	The grace of our Lord, etc.
And they reply:	Amen.
And the priest says:	Lift up your minds (May your minds be above).
And they reply:	Towards you, O God.
And the priest says:	The oblation is offered to God the Lord of all.
And they reply:	It is fit and right.
And the deacon says:	Peace be with us.

B

And the priest recites quietly:
Worthy of praise from every mouth, and thanksgiving from every tongue
is the adorable and glorious Name of the Father and the Son and of the
Holy Spirit, who created the world by his grace and its inhabitants in his
compassion, and redeemed mankind in his mercy, and has effected [lit.
made] great grace towards mortals.

NOTES A

2. And with you/ B.D.F.I.O.P.R.W.Z.b.c.f.h. . . . l.n.p.t.u. **a.b.c.d.e.f.h.i.j.k.l.** *Mb. Tr. Mn.*
   With you   A.C.E.H.J.K.T.U.Y. e.a. *CH* (except f.g.h.l.) v.w.z. *Cr. Re.* **g.**
3. Give/ Give (singular) I.O. **b.k.**
   READ my brothers give, x.y. *Cr. Mb.*
4. Catholikoi/: READ Patriarchs (the pointing indicates that the plural is intended) **j.**
   With the pointing, K. *Mb.* 1774.
5. and intercede/ ADD and pray I.J.a. *Cr.* (This would seem to be merely a continuation
   of the prayer).
6. THE FULL TEXT OF MANY Mss. READS. The grace of our Lord Jesus Christ, and
   the love of God the Father, and the fellowship of the Holy Spirit be with us all,
   now and at all times, and for ever and ever.
7. *And they reply:* Amen/OM. H.J.a.j.w.
9. THE FULL TEXT IN MANY Mss. READS. *And they reply:* Towards you, O God of
   Abraham and of Isaac and of Israel, O glorious king.
10. to God/ ADD: the exalted D.

14

In addition, the following readings have been added to the apparatus by Douglas Webb:

a	Rylands Library, Manchester, Syr. 19	.. .. ..	1604
b	Chald. Patr. Mosul 280/281	.. .. ..	1670
c	Bibliotheque Nationale, Paris. Syr. 283	.. .. ..	1684
d	Cambr. Add. 1984	.. ..	1707
e	Bibliotheque Nationale, Paris Syr. 310	.. .. ..	1744
f	Bibliotheque Nationale, Paris Syr. 96	.. .. ..	1699
g	Bodleian Oxford, Ouseley 267	.. ..	18th ?
	(Bilingual, Syriac-Latin, the Syriac being Chaldean, and the Latin a carelessly applied version of the Malabar rite)		
h	Vat. Syr. 291	.. ..	1776
i	Bibliotheque Nationale, Paris Syr. 90	.. .. ..	1698
j	Vat. Syr. 290	.. .. ..	prior to 1751
k	Leiden, Or. 1215	.. .. ..	prior to 1720
l	Bibliotheque Nationale, Paris Syr. 88	.. .. ..	18th ?

TEXT—*SHARAR*

[The opening dialogue of *Sharar*, which is followed by a blessing of the congregation, and a prayer relating to incense, and commemorations, has few obvious parallels with **AM**, particularly the abbreviated form of the Mar Esa'ya text, and *pace* Macomber, hardly provides a basis for a reconstruction of an original common text. After the commemorations the anaphora recommences. For the use of underlining see page 13].

B

He inclines to the right and to the left of the altar. And he begins the anaphora of Peter the Apostle.
Bowing:
Glory to you, the adorable and glorious Name of the Father and of the Son, and of the Holy Spirit, who created the worlds by your grace and its inhabitants in your mercy; and has effected [lit. made] redemption for mortals by your grace.

NOTES *B*

2. tongue/ A.B.C.F.G.N.
   ADD and adoration and worship from every creature I.J.K.O. *AQ* (except c.s.u.v.) W.X. (deficit post every) *ML.* a.z. *CH. Edd. Mn. Re.*
   ADD and adoration from every creature D.E.W. *ibid.,* BUT mouth FOR creature T.e.
   READ and adoration and glory and exaltation P.s.u.v.
   OMIT creature AND READ which is created and fashioned in heaven and on earth. H.
3. and glorious/ A. . . . K.N.P.T.V. (but ms. deficit) W.a.j.z. *Re. Sr.*
   ADD of the glorious Trinity O.R.S.U.Y. *ML.* b . . . e. *CH* (except x.y.) in (2a manu) *Cr.Mb.Mn.*
   of the Father/ Father n. (2a manu) p.s. . . . w. *Cm.*
   and the Son/ and the Son and of the (Holy) Spirit A.O.S.
   and of the Son and of the (Holy) Spirit. N.R. b.d.g. . . . i.l.m.o.q.r. *Cr. Sr.*
   and the son and in the (Holy) Spirit. ceteri.
4. world/ Worlds G.T. q.y. *Sr.*
5. in his mercy mankind (mere inversion) O.
6. great/ OM. B.I. (In H. great is masculine, presumably a scribal error).

15

C

Your majesty, O Lord, a thousand thousand heavenly beings worship and myriad myriads of angels, hosts of spiritual beings, ministers (of) fire and of spirit, with cherubim and ho:y seraphim, glorify your Name
Qanona. Crying out and glorifying
And they reply: Holy, Holy.

D

And the priest recites quietly:
And with these heavenly powers we give thanks to you, O Lord, even we, your lowly, weak and miserable servants, because you have effected in us a great grace which cannot be repaid, in that you put on our humanity so as to quicken us by your divinity. And you lifted up our poor estate, and righted our fall. And you raised up our mortality. And you forgave our debts. You justified our sinfulness and you enlightened our understanding. And you, our Lord and our God, vanquished our enemies and made triumphant the lowliness of our weak nature through the abounding compassion of your grace.
Qanona. And for all
And they reply: Amen.
And the deacon says: In your minds.

NOTES *C*

1. heavenly beings/ OMIT V. READ spiritual beings A. heavenly angels *Sr*
    worship/ A.B.F.N.T. *CH* (except g.q.)
    worship and bow down q. bow down and worship, ceteri.
2. myriads/ (a *nun* is not in the Mar Esa'ya text. It is perhaps illegible, or a scribal error).
    of angels/ ADD sanctifying, B.E.G.N.
        READ holy angels, ceteri. of holy angels and archangels D.
    hosts/ of hosts, ceteri.
    of spiritual beings/ OMIT C. I *Sr.*
    ministers/ OMIT C. and ministers E.G.T.V.Y. of ministers I *Sr*
2-3. hosts . . . cherubim/ OM. per haplog. J.
3. and of spirit/ H.K. *Re.* ADD sanctify your Name, I.P.V.W.a.j.z. glorify your name
        ceteri. glorify in fear, *Sr*, in fear and trembling glorify, I
    with/ A.B.C.F.G.H.U.T.e.g.w. *Ur. Re. Sr.* and with, ceteri.
        cherubim/A.B.F.G.N. ADD holy ceteri.
    holy seraphim/ A.B.F.G.N. OMIT holy, *Mn. Sr.* spiritual seraphim, ceteri.
    glorify your Name/ OMIT A.B F.G.N. READ sanctify and honour your Name, H.
        sanctify and praise your Name, K. I *Re.* offering worship without ceasing to your
        Lordship, V. offering worship without ceasing and everlastingly to your Lord-
        ship, C. offering worship to your Lordship, ceteri (and . . . J).
4. *Qanona*/ OMIT E, (but in margin). B.
    and glorifying/ OMIT G.
        ADD, calling to one another without ceasing, and saying, A-F. H-K.
        O.P.Q.R.U.V.W.Y.a.b.e.g.h.i.j.l.p.t.u.v.w.**a.b.c.d.e.f.g.h.i.j.k.** *Cr CM. Mb. Ur*
5. Holy, Holy,/ G H I.K.N.O.P. OMIT one 'Holy' *Mb.* 1778
    ADD etc., A.E.G.I.e. Holy, Lord God of Hosts, heaven and earth are full of his glory.
        B C. (but omit one 'holy') D.v.**h.** *ibid.,* BUT ADD etc. W.Y. Holy J.O.a.g. Holy.
        etc., R.U.b.h.i.j.l.p.t.u.v. **a.b.c.d.e.** Cr.
    READ Holy, Holy, Holy, Lord God of Hosts, heaven and earth are full of his glories:
        Hosanna in the highest. Hosanna to the Son of David. Blessed is he who
        came and who comes in the Name of the Lord. Hosanna in Highest. w. **g.i.**
        Cm. (1901).
    READ AS ABOVE, BUT AFTER glories ADD and of the nature of his being, and of
        the excellency of his glorious splendour. Hosanna (as above) *Ur.*
    ADD Holy, Lord of Hosts, etc., I

C

And he raises his voice and extends his hands, and says:
Your majesty, O Lord, a thousand thousand heavenly angels worship and myriad myriads of hosts of ministers of fire and of spirit glorify in fear. With the cherubim and seraphim, who from one to another bless and sanctify and cry out and say

May we also, O Lord, through your grace and your compassion be made worthy to say with them 3 Times
Holy, Holy, Holy.

D

The priest inclines:
We give thanks to you, O Lord, we your sinful servants because you have effected in us your grace which cannot be repaid. You put on our humanity so as to quicken us by your divinity. You lifted up our poverty and righted our dejection. And you quickened our mortality, and you justified our sinfulness and you forgave our debts. And you enlightened our understanding, and vanquished our enemies and made triumphant our lowliness.

And he raises his voice saying:
And for all your graces towards us, let us offer to you glory, and honour in your holy church before your propitiatory altar, now . . .

NOTES D

2. give thanks/ worship, W.
   even/ OMIT T. *Sr.*
3. in us/ OMIT A.
4. in that you put on/ that you did put on, A.
6. And you raised up our mortality/ OMIT O. *CH. Cr.*
8-9. and made triumphant/ made triumphant, U. ADD our Lord, *Mb.*
10. of your grace/ B.R.U.W.Y.a.b.e.g. . . . .j.l.p.t.u.v.w. **b.c.d.e.f.h.i.j.k.** *Cm.Mb.* 1778 *Ur.*
    ADD O merciful One, and pardoner of debts, A.D.
       O merciful One, and pardoner of debts and sins, and forgive me my debts. C
       ibid., BUT OMIT sins AND ADD in the Judgment, K.P.
       O merciful One, and pardoner of debts and sins, forgive me my debts and sins in your love, E. **g.**
       O merciful One, and pardoner of debts, forgive me my sins and debts in the Judgment. **a**
       O merciful One, and pardoner of debts and sins, forgive me my debts and sins in the Judgment, and the sins of my fathers in the Judgment. V.
    OMIT THE ENTIRE GEHANTA **I**
11. all/ ADD your aids and graces towards us let us offer to you glory, and honour, and thanksgiving, and worship, now, A.C.F.G.I.J.P.R.U.W. a.b.h.i.j.l.p.u.v. **a.b.c.d.e.f.h.**
    ibid., — and at all times, V.Y.t. **j.h.**
    ibid., — and at all times and for ever and ever. D.E.H.K.O. e.w. **g.l.**
12. *And they reply:* Amen./ OMIT D.F.G.H.J.K.L.M.N. *AQ* (except n.p.s.u.) T.X. *ML.*
    a.z. OMIT *And they reply: Cm.*
13. In your minds./ ADD Pray, Peace be with us. B.C.D.H.I.J.N.V.W.
    ADD be standing and praying, Peace be with us. i. (In **j** 'in your minds' is given to the priest and not the deacon).

17

E

And the priest recites quietly:
You, O Lord, in your unspeakable mercies make a gracious remembrance for all the upright and just fathers who have been pleasing before you in the commemoration of the body and blood of your Christ which we offer to you upon the pure and holy altar as you have taught us. And grant us your tranquillity and your peace all the days of the world. Repeat.
And they reply: Amen.

NOTES E

2. your unspeakable mercies/ in marg. 2a manu, many. In textu, ceteri; many mercies, *Sr.*
    unspeakable/ ADD repeat. B.C.H.I.J.K.O.P.U.V.W.Y. a.b.e.g.j.p.t.u.v. **a.b.c.d.e.f.**
    make/ make us worthy that we may make, *Cm* 1901
    gracious/ *Sr.* ADD and acceptable. ceteri. OMIT gracious, D
    for all/ praem. to the virgin Mary, Mother of God and. m.o.q.r.x.y. *Cr. Mb.* [but not, apparently, in the mss. of the Malabar rite] (omit and).

3. who have been pleasing before you/ OMIT G.

5. altar/ A-F.L.N.T.X.z. *Mn.*
    his altar, J.a.
    your altar, ceteri, *Sr.*
    as you have taught us/ as he has taught us, C.
    and grant ... Amen/ READ, Yea, Our Lord and our God, repeat, grant us your health and your peace all the days of the world. A.C.H.

6. repeat ... Amen./ OMIT K.L.N. *ML.* **i.** *Mb.*
    OMIT AND READ Repeat, 3 times: Yea and Amen. E.T. (omit times). Yea and Amen, Repeat, 3 times. w.
    OMIT AND READ Yea, our Lord and our God, grant us your health and your peace all the days of the world. V.Y.o.r. **g.j.k.**
    OMIT and your peace, ... world, *Mn.*
    OMIT AND READ Repeat, Yea, our Lord and our God grant us your health and your peace all the days of the world. x. *Cr. Re.* (omit Yea) **f. h.**
    OMIT AND READ Yea, our Lord and our God, Grant us your health and your peace all the days of the world. Repeat. S.U.b.c.i.m.n.q.u.y. *Tr. Cm.* **a.b.c.d.e.**
    OMIT AND READ Yea, our Lord and our God. Repeat, Grant us your health and your peace all the days of the world. D.I.J.P.Q.W.a.j.z.
    (These variants arise from the scribes' interpretation of the rubric 'Repeat')

1-7. OMIT THE WHOLE GEHANTA I.

---

continued from page 19 opposite]

May the glorious Trinity be pleased by this incense and by this oblation and by this chalice; and may the souls be absolved by it and the spirits be sanctified by it for whom and on behalf of whom it was offered and sanctified. And upon me, feeble and sinful, who offered it, may the mercy of the glorious Trinity shine forth, Father . . .

He bows to the right and to the left of the altar, and invokes the mother of God, to his aid, and says the prayer of inclination:
Mother of our Lord Jesus Christ, pray for me to your only begotten son, who was born from you, that he will pardon my debts and sins: and receive from my lowly* and sinful hands this oblation which my weakness* offers upon this holy altar of Mar N . . . through your intercession for us, Holy Mother.

E

Bowing.

You, O Lord, therefore, in your many mercies make a gracious remembrance for all the upright and just fathers in the commemoration of your body and your blood which we offer to you upon your living and holy altar as you, our hope, have taught us in your holy gospel and have said 'I am the bread of life which came down from heaven so that mortals may have life in me'.

And he raises his voice

We make, O Lord, the memorial of your passion as you have taught us: In that night when you were delivered up to the crucifiers, O Lord, you took bread in your pure and holy hands, and you looked to heaven to your glorious Father. You blessed, and signed, hallowed, O Lord, and broke and gave to your disciples, the blessed apostles, and said to them, 'This bread is my body which is broken and given for the life of the world, and for those who take it, for the pardon of debts and forgiveness of sins. Take, eat from it, and it will be to you for eternal life'.

And he takes the cup and says

And likewise over the cup you gave thanks and glorified and said, O Lord, 'This cup is my blood of the New Testament which is shed for many for the remission of sins. Take, drink from it all of you, and it will be to you for the pardon of debts and forgiveness of sins and eternal life'. Amen.

And he says:

For whenever you eat from this holy body and drink from this cup of life and salvation you are calling to remembrance the death and resurrection of your Lord until the great day of his coming.

People: Your death, O Lord, we call to remembrance.

Priest:

We remember you, only-begotten of the Father, firstborn of Being, spiritual lamb, who descended from on high to below to be a propitirtory sacrifice for all mankind to take away their sins voluntarily, and to pardon sinners through your blood and to sanctify the unclean through your sacrifice. Make us live, O Lord, through your true life, purify us through your spiritual expiation, and grant us that we may obtain life by your life-giving death, and that we may stand before you in purity, and serve you in holines and offer this oblation to your divinity; that the will of your majesty may be pleased by it, and your mercy flow out upon us all, Father . . .

Yes, we beg you, only-begotten of the Father, through whom peace has been proclaimed to us, Child of the Most High by whom the things above were reconciled with the things below, 'The Good Shepherd who laid himself down for his sheep and delivered them from ravening wolves', merciful Lord, who cried out on the cross and gathered us from the error of vanity:: El, God of spirits and of all flesh, may our prayers be lifted up to you and your mercy descend on our petitions, and may this oblation be acceptable before you; which we offer on your atoning altar in memory of your passion. May it please your divinity, and your will be fulfilled by it; and our debts pardoned by it, and our sins forgiven by it; and by it our dead commemorated; and let us confess and worship and glorify you, and your Father who sent you for our salvation, and your living and Holy Spirit. Now . . .

[continued at foot of page 18 opposite

19

F

That all the inhabitants of the earth may know that you alone are God, the true Father, and you have sent our Lord Jesus Christ, your Son and your beloved, and he, our Lord and our God, taught us in his life-giving gospel all the purity and holiness of the prophets, apostles, martyrs and confessors and bishops and priests and deacons, and of all the children of the holy catholic church, who have been marked with the mark of holy baptism.

G

And we also, O Lord,—3 Times—your lowly, weak and miserable servants who are gathered together and stand before you at this time have received by tradition of the example which is from you rejoicing, and glorifying, and magnifying, and commemorating and praising, and performing this great and dread mystery of the passion and death and resurrection of our Lord Jesus Christ.

NOTES *F*

2. Father/ OMIT A.G. *Cm.*
   your Son/ OMIT F. la manu.
2-3. your beloved/the beloved. *Cm.* 1936.
3. and he/ namely, that is to say, A.E.T.
   our Lord and our God/ OMIT A.
   taught us/ taught us, B.D.I.K.N.O. (merely constructional difference).
   who taught us. A.
   who came and taught us, T.
   came and taught us, ceteri.
   in his life-giving gospel/ OMIT O. *Ch. Cr. Re.*
4. the purity/ praem. honour and, K.
   vitality, C.
   and holiness/ OMIT L.
4-5. of the prophets . . . and of all/ SUBSTITUTE to FOR of, T.
5. and bishops/ A. L. praem. and doctors, B.F.H.K.T.V.k.w. *Mb.* idem. sed interv.
   ceteri, except I; praeterea. praem. and of Patriarchs, i.
6. catholic church/ INSERT and when he says 'those who have been marked', let him sign from below, and from right to left as he bows. And the priest rises and raising his hands upwards: and the deacon says, In silence and in awe: who have been marked. Y.
   who have been marked/ who has been marked, C.
   with the mark/ *Sr.* ADD in marg. 2a manu, living.
   in textu, B.C.D.F.G.H.J.K.O. a. *CH.* w.z. *Cr. Tr. Cm.* **a.b.c.d.e.f.h.**
   praeterea, ADD lifegiving ('living and lifegiving') E.I.M.P.O. W.*ML. Mb* 1778 **g.i.j.k.**
   READ lifegiving, A.L.T. READ holy (with the holy mark) N.
1-6. OMIT THE ENTIRE SECTION R. (defective ms.).

NOTES *G*

1-5. And we also . . . dread. OMIT R. (defective ms.)
1. O Lord/ OMIT L **f**
   thrice/ praem. repeat, *AQ.* (except R.t.) W. *ML.*g.w.z. *Mb. Tr. Cm.* **b.c.d.e.h.**
   OMIT AND READ Repeat, A.B.C.F.J.K.O.V.a. *Ch.* (excepting g) t. *Cr. Re.* **a.f.g.i.j.**
   OMIT D.E.G.H.I.L.M.N.P.Q.T.
   your servants/ ADD Repeat, G.
   and miserable/ praeterea, ADD Repeat, D. (Implicite). I.M.N.P.Q.
2. who are gathered together A. ADD in your Name, ceteri.
   at this time/ OMIT A.B.C.F.H.N. OMIT this, Y.
   have received/ Y.b. and have received, ceteri.
3. by tradition of the example/ example and tradition A.
   by tradition the example, ceteri.
   from you/ from your Son, *Cm.*
   rejoicing/ praem. and, E.r. rejoicing and exulting ,B.C.F.

F

Inclining:
We offer before you, O Lord, this oblation in memory of all the upright and just fathers, prophets and apostles and martyrs and confessors; and of all our patriarchs, the Pope of the city of Rome and Metropolitan, bishops, chorepiscopei, periodentai, *priests, and deacons,* and deaconesses, young men, celibates, virgins, and all of the children of the holy church who are marked with the mark of saving baptism and whom you have made to participate in your holy body.
And he says quietly:
But especially and first of all we commemorate the holy and saintly and blessed Virgin Mary, the blessed mother of God.
Deacon: Remember her, O Lord God, and us through her pure prayers.
The priest inclines:
Remember, O Lord God, at this moment those far off, and those present, the dead and the living, the sick and the oppressed, the distressed and the afflicted, and those who are in various troubles.
Remember, O Lord God, at this moment, our fathers and our brothers in spirit and flesh; and pardon their debts and their sins.
Remember, O Lord God, at this moment those who offer oblations, vows, firstfruits and memorials. Grant to their petitions good things from your abundant treasure.
Remember, O Lord God, at this moment those who partake in commemorating your holy mother and your saints. Grant them recompense with a good reward. And for all who participated in this Eucharist which was offered upon this holy altar. Grant them, O Lord God, a good reward in your kingdom. And for all those who have said to us 'Remember us in your prayers because of our Lord', remember them, O God, and pardon their faults.
Remember, O Lord God, at this moment, my miserableness, my sinfulness, my importunity and my lowliness, I who wittingly or unwittingly, freely or involuntarily, have sinned and committed evil before you. O Lord God, in your grace and mercy pardon and forgive me whatever I have sinned against you; and O Lord, may this Eucharist be as a memorial of our dead and for the pardon of our souls.
Remember, O Lord God, at this time, your sickly and sinful servant George, who wrote (this). And pardon and forgive his debts and his sins, and pardon his fathers. Amen.

4.   and magnifying/ OMIT I.M.P.Q. *ML. Mb.* ADD, and praising, V.
and commemorating/ and calling to mind A.C. Transplante and magnifying, x.y. *Cr.*
and praising/ OMIT ceteri.
and performing/ performing, *Cm.*
this (lit. it) OMIT T. ('it' is merely the pronoun standing as the object of the verb).
and dread/ B.F.L. OMIT AND READ holy and divine, A.
dread/ READ dread, and holy and divine, C.D.G.H.J.K.N.O.a. *CH.* (except x.)
   Cr. Mn. Re. (**a.** a supply page) **f.g.**
      praeterea, ADD, and lifegiving, AFTER holy, I.M.P.Q.R. (deficit usque and
         lifegiving). *AQ.* V.W. *ML.* x.z. *Mb. Tr. Cm.* **b.c.d.h.i.**
   READ SIMPLY holy and glorious, E.
   READ and glorious and holy and lifegiving and divine, T.w.
and death/ L.N.W.j.o.p. (la manu) v.w. ADD and burial, ceteri.
5-6.   of our Lord Jesus/ A.B.C.E.F.G.J.L.N.T. a.w. ADD and Saviour, ceteri (OMIT and
   Ur.).

H

May he come, O Lord, your Holy Spirit and rest upon this oblation *(of)*

And the deacon says: Be in silence:

of your servants, and bless and hallow it, that it may be to us, O Lord, for the pardon of debts and the forgiveness of sins, and a great hope of resurrection from the dead and a new life in the kingdom of heaven with all who have been pleasing before you.

I

And for all your marvellous economy towards us we give you thanks and praise you without ceasing in your Church redeemed by the precious blood of your Christ, with open mouths and with uncovered faces.

Qanona. As we offer up

And they reply: Amen.

And they conclude everything as it is written in the Anaphora of the Interpreter, which (?) is written (?) (holy?) Sunday of the Annunciation.

NOTES *H*

1. May he come/ J.a. (la manu) x. *Cr.*
   And may she come, E.P. (merely a question of grammar, as the Syriac word for 'Spirit' is feminine).
   And may he come, ceteri.
   your Holy Spirit/ the Spirit of holiness, and dwell, H.
   your living and Holy Spirit, C.E.J.K.Y.a.z. **a.** *Sr.*
   and rest upon/ ADD and dwell, O
   (of) (The scribe evidently started to write 'of your servants' and then decided to insert the deacon's exclamation, failing to delete the *dalat,* 'of')

2. *And the deacon . . .* silence:/ OMIT A C D F.G.H.O.K.L.N.P.R.S.U.V.c.h.l.m.w. *Re.*
   in silence/ ADD and dread, B.E.H.J.O.W.Y.b.i.j.n.p.t.u.v.w.z.
   Edd. **b.c.d.e.**
   idem, et praem. and, J.a.e. **a.**

5-6. with all . . . before you/ OMIT C.H. *Mn.*

6. before you/ before him, O.T. *CH.* (except r.x.) *Cr. Re.* **f.g.h.k.**
   praeterea, ADD by his grace, r.
   And for/for, A.
   marvellous/A-F.H.J.N.O.T.V. a. *CH.* w.z. *Cr. Mn. Re.*
   praem. this great (and) G.I.L.M. *AQ.* (except Y.u.) W. *ML. Mb. Tr. Cm.* **i.j.k.**
   OMIT AND READ, glorious, P. praem. this, Y.
   your . . . economy/ A. . . . D.F.H.J.K.N.O.a. *CH* (except q) w.z. *Cr. Mn. Re. Sr.* **f. g.**
   the . . . economy, ceteri. (**a** reads 'your economy', followed by 'great and marvellous', but it is on a supply page. The original was presumably 'this great and marvellous economy').

H

He kneels and calls the Spirit saying:

Hear me, O Lord. Hear me, O Lord. Hear me, O Lord. <u>And may he come, O
Lord, your living and Holy Spirit, and dwell</u> and rest <u>upon this oblation of
your servants. And</u> may it <u>to be</u> those who partake <u>for the pardon of debts
and the forgiveness of sins and</u> for a blessed <u>resurrection from the dead
and a new life in the kingdom of heaven</u> for ever.

I

And he raises his voice:

<u>And for your glorious economy towards us we give you thanks,</u> we your
sinful servants, <u>redeemed by your</u> innocent <u>blood, with open mouth</u> which
gives thanks in <u>your holy church</u> before your propitiatory altar, <u>now</u> . . .

NOTES *I*

2. without ceasing/ OMIT P.
    your church/ the church, J.
    the blood/ your blood, B. (According to Macomber, I (la manu), but Douglas
        Webb can find no trace of the alteration on his microfilm of this text).
3. of your Christ/ of Christ, A.
    and with . . . faces/ and . . . faces, C.J.
    add, Repeat, E.H.W. **a.**
    Ibid., sed post ceasing **i.j.k.**
4. *Qanona.* As we offer up/ READ *Qanona.* As we offer up glory and honour and
    thanksgiving and worship to your living and holy and life-giving Name,
    now. *And he signs* upon the mysteries. *And they reply:* Amen. A.C.G.I.J.
    M.P.R.W.a.b.g.h.i.j.p.t.v. **a.b.c.d.e.f.**
    Ibid., BUT AFTER now ADD and at all times and for ever and ever,
        B.D.H.K.O.V.b.w. **i.**
    OMIT to your living, holy and life-giving Name, now and at all times for
        ever and ever, E
    OMIT ALL AFTER 'glory', N.
    OMIT and at all times and for ever and ever. b.
    OMIT, and for ever and ever, F.U.Y. **j.k.**
    OMIT *Qanona.,* AND READ *And raising his voice,* AND AFTER life-giving,
        READ *and he signs over the cup and the dish, and he says:* now and at all
        times and for ever and ever. Amen. **g.**
5. *And they reply:* Amen/ OMIT F.G.H.L.N. *CH.* (except h.l.) **f.h.**
1-7. And for . . . Amen/ OMIT ENTIRE SECTION (defective ms.) u.

COMMENTARY

Structure

Recent studies on the origin and structure of the eucharistic prayer have taken as their starting point the Jewish *berakoth,* and in particular, the table prayers of the *Birkat ha-mazon,* and the themes of the *tephilla,* or 18 benedictions. The structure of the Jewish *berakoth* has also been the subject of study. According to Audet, they are of two types—formal and informal.[1] The latter commence with the benedictional formula ('Blessed are you, O Lord') and then give the reason for the benediction; the former have in addition a closing formula. However, both Robert Ledogar and Thomas Talley have drawn attention to the fact that when *berakoth* occur in a series, only the first begins with the benedictional formula, but all conclude with a *chatimah,* or doxology.[2]

According to many scholars, **AM** is based directly upon the pattern of Jewish *berakoth,* and, like the *Didache* 10, has a tripartite structure reflecting the *Birkat ha-mazon;* it consists of three *gehantas,* each concluding with a *qanona.*[3] However, it is also possible to see **AM** as having a bipartite structure, marked by the two doxologies; as Emmanual Cutrone has observed, with the exception of the sequence intercessions-epiklesis, a bipartite structure corresponds to the eucharistic prayer outlined in the *Mystagogic Catecheses* attributed to Cyril of Jerusalem.[4]

A (Prefatory dialogue)

Macomber has argued that the present dialogue has no connection with paragraph *B;* the final acclamation in the dialogue prefatory to the solemn blessing of baptismal oil does, and he suggested that the latter originally belonged to the eucharistic anaphora, finding some (though not particularly strong) support in the dialogue of *Sharar.*[5] Ledogar also remarks that the usual 'Let us give thanks to the Lord' may have been replaced in the Nestorian rite by 'The Oblation is being offered to God the Lord of all'.[6] However, as we shall suggest below, oblation may be a Syrian equivalent of thanksgiving.

B

Unlike the anaphoras of the West Syrian tradition, **AM** is extremely economic in its opening praise vocabulary. It combines two distinct

---

[1] J. P. Audet, 'Literary Forms and Contents of a Normal Eucharistia in the First Century' in *Text und Untersuchungen* 73 (Berlin, 1959) pp.643-662; J. Heinemann, *Prayer in the Talmud.*

[2] Robert J. Ledogar *Acknowledgment: Praise Verbs in the Early Greek Anaphoras* (Herder, Rome 1968) pp.121-124. T. J. Talley, 'The Eucharistic Prayer of the Ancient Church According to Recent Research', pp.139-142.

[3] E.g. T. J. Talley *art. cit.;* Sanchez Caro *art. cit.*

[4] E. J. Cutrone, 'Cyril's Mystagogical Catecheses and the evolution of the Jerusalem Anaphora' in *OCP* 44 (1978), pp.52-64.

[5] W. F. Macomber, 'The Maronite and Chaldean Versions of the Anaphora of the Apostles'.

[6] Ledogar *op. cit.,* p.27.

praise notions, which, in the view of Ledogar, were connected with the eucharist in the primitive church: the act of proclaiming the name of Jesus-Kurios as a profession of faith in him, and the expression of gratitude for the privilege of belonging to the community of those who 'glory' in the name of Jesus.[1] Its form recalls the *Qaddis* of the Synagogue liturgy which blesses the divine name, the nucleus of which probably dates from the Tannaitic period.[2] The blessing of the name also occurs in a more diffused form in the *Yotser or*.

In Philippians 2.11 the name is revealed as Jesus-Kurios. In Malachi 1.11 it is to the name that a pure offering is made, and this text is mentioned in he *Didache* and by Justin Martyr. In the former, the pure offering appears to be the Christian's offering of himself, his heart and conscience, while in Justin it includes the eucharistic bread and wine. We also find what seems to be an allusion to Malachi in the Syrian *Odes of Solomon:*

> I am a priest of the Lord
> And him I serve as a priest;
> And to him I offer the oblation of his thoughts.
> . . .
> The oblation of the Lord is righteousness
> And purity of heart and lips.[3]

It is not impossible that 'to offer the oblation' is the Syrian equivalent of *eucharistesomen to kurio* of the Greek anaphoras, and refers to acknowledgment and praise of the name, the Christ who reveals himself in the breaking of the bread. If this were the case, then there is a quite logical connection between the dialogue and this paragraph.

It is difficult to decide whether or not *Sharar* here preserves an earlier form. However, nearly all reconstructions regard the 'Trinitarian' reference as a later addition, explaining it as an anti-Arian measure. Although the variant readings of **AM** where the Trinity is explicitly mentioned must be regarded as later interpolations, there seems to be no convincing reason for excising the reference to Father, Son and Holy Spirit, which is common to both texts. It can hardly be maintained that Matthew 28.19—a document to which modern scholarship assigns a Jewish-Christian provenance—was originally said or written as an anti-Arian measure, or with a Constantinopolitan doctrine of the Trinity in mind! One modern commentator takes the Matthean text as an expansion of baptism 'in the name of Christ', and having the meaning' in the name of Christ who was sent by God and who himself baptizes with the Holy Spirit now being poured out on all flesh'.[4] Quite probably this reflects liturgical usage. Accordingly, the reference in **AM** can be no more out of place than is the reference in Matthew. Christians believed that the name had been revealed through the work of the Son in the Holy Spirit, and there is no need to regard the reference in **AM** as having any more meaning than that.

[1] *Ibid.*, p.153.
[2] Heinemann *op. cit.*, p.256.
[3] *The Odes of Solomon*, ed. J. H. Charlesworth (OUP 1973).
[4] M. Barth, *Die Taufe, ein Sakrament?* (Evangelischor Verlag, Zurich, 1951), p.552.

C (Sanctus)

A formidable number of scholars have followed Ratcliff in regarding the sanctus and its introduction as an intrusion into the text which should be deleted. Nevertheless, it is common to both **AM** and *Sharar;* is it, therefore, an intrusion?

AM praises the name of God who created the world(s) and its inhabitants; *Sharar* gives glory to the name who created the worlds and its inhabitants. God is creator of heaven and earth, the heavenly world and the lower earthly world (perhaps a variant reading of *Sharar,* 'their inhabitants', is to be preferred). In heaven the name is worshipped without ceasing, and the sanctus is a quite logical inclusion, since it is the 'glory' which the inhabitants of the heavenly world continually offer to God. Then follows the thanksgiving of mortals. If this is correct, the sanctus is certainly no intrusion, and it is possible that underlying the thought here is the Syrian conception of the different levels of the mountain of paradise, with the *shekinah* of God at the summit.[1]

The sanctus may have entered the anaphora under the influence of the *Qedussah* of the Synagogue, or the *Yorde Merkabah* mystical tradition, whose hymns invariably terminated with *Qedussah.*[2] The angelology of **AM** is very restrained in comparison with the elaborate hierarchy found in anaphoras such as that of St. James.

D

If the sanctus is an elaboration of the glory offered by the higher heavenly world, the anaphora proceeds now to explain why glory can be offered by mankind. The words 'lowly, weak and miserable', which also occur in paragraph *G,* and are found in the anamnesis of *Theodore,* and at the introduction to the epiklesis in *Nestorius,* have no parallel in *Sharar* (though similar phraseology does occur later in the private *mementos* of the priest), and it may be that these words represent a devotional or liturgical phrase peculiar to the East Syrians.[3]

Robert Murray points out that in most Syriac writings extant from the third and fourth centuries, it can be said that 'he clothed himself with a body' is the standard expression for the incarnation. The expression is found frequently in the Acts of Judas Thomas, almost always in prayers; the Son 'put on' the body, humanity, or the first man.[4] Herman Wegman has commented:

> '**AM** describes here the Syriac way of believing: the incarnation is dressing oneself with a body, through which Jesus can give new life, a new body. The deliverence is salvation to life, which we receive from him, who became "adam" and dressed himself with his body.'[5]

[1] R. Murray, *Symbols of Church and Kingdem,* p.258.

[2] See further, Bryan D. Spinks, 'The Jewish Sources for the Sanctus' in *The Heythrop Journal* 21 (1980), pp.168-179.

[3] cf. Ephraem: 'humanity was weak, suffering and fainting; thou hast strengthened it with thy blessed Bread, thou hast consoled it with thy sober wine, and thou hast given it joy with thy holy anointing.'

[4] Murray, *op. cit.,* p.311.

[5] Wegman, *art. cit.,* p.34.

The paragraph ends with a doxology, which, as Ratcliff observed, effectively divides the anaphora into two distinct parts. However, there is no need to follow Ratcliff in assuming it to be an interpolation. On analogy with the Jewish *berakoth,* there is no reason to believe that a eucharistic prayer was one continuous prayer with only one final doxology.

E

E raises the question of the place of intercession. While the absence of the *cushapa* intercessions from the Mar Esa'ya text have been taken as confirmation that these were a later intrusion into the prayer, intercessory material is present in the *gehantas,* in paragraphs *E* and *F.* In this paragraph God is asked to remember the 'upright and just fathers', and to grant tranquillity and peace. The identity of the 'fathers' is far from clear. If we consider Ephraem's use of words, then the 'just' are those who take the middle position on the mountain of paradise.[1] Possibly, therefore, it refers to the martyrs. The 'fathers' are also remembered in the *Ahabah* before *Shema* in the Synagogue liturgy, and the same prayer also asks for peace; remembrance of the fathers also occurs in embolisms in the *Birkat hamazon.* In **AM** the object of the remembrance seems to be to associate those who have died with the thanksgiving of angels and men; behind the words of the prayer there seems to be a vision of a cosmic act of praise and thanksgiving in which all creation shares—angels, mankind, and those who have died. The remembrance in **AM** is linked with the 'commemoration of the body and blood of your Christ'. It would seem likely that the root *'hd,* commemoration, should be understood as proclamation, or praise.[2] Accordingly the eucharistic action is regarded as a sacrifice of praise.

Whereas in **AM** the paragraph concludes with a petition for peace, *Sharar* concludes with a Johannine quotation, and at this point introduces an institution narrative which is addressed to the Son. Macomber, Sanchez Caro and Wegman have all considered this to be the 'missing' narrative of **AM,** and have incorporated it into their reconstructions.

In favour of its originality, the narrative of *Sharar* has some peculiar characteristics, and in particular, it has the term 'the crucifiers', *zoqopa,* which with *saloba,* also meaning 'crucifier', is used by Ephraem as a synonym for the Jews.[3] Furthermore, the asymmetry of the narrative may point to an early date, and there is no precedent for a narrative within intercessions for the departed. On the other hand, lack of symmetry is a characteristic of some late West Syrian anaphoras, and it is also strange, that, while one of the characteristics of **AM** is the lack of lengthy biblical quotations, *Sharar* uses a lengthy quotation to introduce the narrative. The strongest argument against its originality is, quite simply, that it is not found in any manuscript of **AM.**

F

Likewise, this is not a true intercessory paragraph, but refers simply to the various ministries in the Church, all of whom are marked with the mark of baptism. The term *rushma,* mark, is a technical term from the Syrian

---

[1] Murray, *op. cit.,* pp.258-9.
[2] Ledogar, *op. cit.,* p.35.
[3] Murray, *op. cit.,* p.41.

baptismal rites, and refers explicitly to the pre-baptismal anointing of the forehead, which in the earliest Syriac texts is associated with ownership and sonship; the Syriac baptismal rite, having the order anointing-baptism, seems to have been patterned on the Jewish rites of circumcision -lustration.[1]

In *Sharar* the ecclesiastical orders and categories are extended, and the prayer is a commemoration for the departed comparable to that described by Cyril of Jerusalem.[2]

G

This paragraph, which has no main verb, is perhaps the most problematical section of **AM**. The whole paragraph is absent from *Sharar,* and this must call in question its authenticity. It may well be a later insertion by an East Syrian redactor, and this possibility is increased by the fact that parallels are found in *Theodore* and *Nestorius,* suggesting these as the source of the interpolation. On the other hand, many scholars have regarded this section as having a primitive 'ring' to it. In addition there is the problem of its identity. The possibilities are summarized by Alphonse Raes:

'It may be an anamnesis; in this case, we may and must postulate a narrative preceding it; . . . It may be also the last part of the Intercession, to which it can be connected without grammatical difficulty. Or it is the prayer of introduction to the epiclesis and we have to add a few words of petition as we find them at this place in the other two anaphoras of the same rite.'[3]

The words 'received by tradition the example (model) which is from you' are clearly a reference to the institution of the eucharist, and one might speculate as to whether there is some connection here with 1 Cor. 11.23, where, underlying Paul's Greek, the Rabbinical technical terms *qibbel,* received, and *masar,* delivered, are used to introduce the institution. Perhaps we have here an East Syrian 'shorthand' narrative of institution. Much of the phraseology of this section recalls the form of an anamnesis; Ledogar is surely correct when he says:

'This text has been the subject of considerable discussion among liturgists, but whatever be its age and original position within the anaphora, there can be little doubt that this composition has all the characteristics of what is usually called an "anamnesis".'[4]

H

While many scholars have regarded an epiklesis as a later refinement to an anaphora, this epiklesis is common to both **AM** and *Sharar,* and has

---

[1] S P Brock, 'The Syrian Baptismal Ordines (with special reference to the anointing)' in *Studia Liturgica* 12 (1977), pp 177-183; 'The Transition to a post-baptismal anointing in the Antiochene rite', forthcoming in ed. Bryan D. Spinks, *The Sacrifice of Praise.*

[2] *Mystagogic Catecheses* 5.9-10.

[3] A. Raes, 'The Enigma of the Chaldean and Malabar Anaphora of the Apostles' in ed. J. Vellian, *The Malabar Church* Orientalia Christiana Analecta 186 (Pont. Institutum Orientalium Studiorum, Rome, 1970), pp.1-8, p.8.

[4] Ledogar, *op. cit.,* p.36.

many 'primitive' hall-marks. An examination of the phraseology of the epiklesis in the classical anaphoras suggests that the use of the verb 'come' is early.[1] 'Bless and hallow' are absent from *Sharar* (though found in the institution narrative), but are found in *Theodore* and *Nestorius,* and it would seem that Botte is quite correct in suggesting that they have been introduced into **AM** from the other two East Syrian anaphoras.[2] 'Dwell', *nesre,* which occurs in *Sharar,* is found in a variant reading of **AM**, and in *Nestorius.* The verb common to **AM** and *Sharar* for the Spirit's activity is 'rest', *nettnih,* and, like 'dwell' in *Sharar,* would seem to derive from Isaiah 11.2 where the Peshitta has these two verbs. If the words 'Bless and hallow' are regarded as an interpolation, then this epiklesis is not consecratory in nature, but asks for the Spirit to rest on the oblation in order that the benefits of communion may be received, and it may be compared with the (controversial) epiklesis in the *Apostolic Tradition* which has a similar focus.

l

Just as the anaphora opened with worship being offered to the name, so it concludes with praise and glory to the revealed name of God. In return for the great economy, or dispensation, into which they have been caught up, the Christian assembly thanks God by praising him and offering in homage this eucharistic prayer in which the economy is recounted. Praise here includes the proclamation of the mighty deeds of God. The whole economy is summed up in the eucharistic bread and wine.[3] The Church can offer this praise with open mouths and uncovered faces (Psalm 51.15; 2 Cor. 3.18), and can raise her voice to sing and proclaim the economy. The eyes of the baptized are opened to observe the mystery of the kingdom, and their tongues are loosened to offer unceasing praise with the 'higher' world of angels. This closing doxology places the celebration in the vision of Revelation 22.3-4: 'There shall no more be anything accursed, but the throne of God and of the Lamb shall be in it, and his servants shall worship him; they shall see his face, and his name shall be on their foreheads'. There is no fear and awe here, but a beholding of the throne of God with open eyes.

---

[1] See S. P. Brock, 'The Epiklesis in the Antiochene Baptismal *Ordines'* in *'Symposium Syriacum 1972'* Orientalis Christiana Analecta 197 (Pont. Institutum Orientalium Studiorum, Rome, 1974), pp.183-215; Bryan D. Spinks, 'The Consecratory Epiklesis in the Anaphora of St. James' in *Studia Liturgica* 11 (1976), pp.19-38.

[2] B. Botte, 'L'epiclese dans les liturgies syriennes orientales', *Sacris Erudiri* 6 (1954), pp.48-72.

[3] Cf. Luther's remark, that the institution narrative is 'a short summary of the whole gospel' (*The Misuse of the Mass,* 1521).

AN INTRODUCTORY NOTE TO THE MANUSCRIPTS BY DOUGLAS WEBB

The student of the Nestorian Liturgies is handicapped from the very outset by the dearth of early manuscript material. He can gain some help from this Commentaries on the rites[1] that have come down to us, but even this help is limited by the fact that we cannot always be absolutely certain as to which of the anaphoras the commentator had in mind. In the list of the Nestorian mss. in *Liturgies Eastern and Western*, F. E. Brightman lists but one prior to the 17th century.[2] In A. Baumstark's *Geschichte der syrischen Literatur*, only 13 early mss. are listed, and of these one or two have perished before transcripts had been made. It is very largely due to the researches of Dr. W. F. Macomber that a large number of early mss. have been brought to light, his most important find being the Mar Esa'ya hudra, which he dated as belonging to the tenth century.

A number of the early manuscripts are of the hudra. In some copies, though by no means all, the three Nestorian anaphoras are to be found, that of **AM** being included among the ceremonies of the Easter Vigil. Hudra mss., however, tend to be very sparse in rubrics, and also abbreviate text, often giving only the *incipits* of the prayers.

The fuller texts of the Liturgy are to be found in the numerous but generally later Missals and Priest's Rituals, and Dr. Macomber has compiled a list of between 150 and 200 mss. which contain one or more of the three anaphoras, though some of them are lost, and few are earlier than the fifteenth century.[3] Dr. Macomber makes the point that the majority of the mss. which he lists belong to what he calls the 'Alqosh tradition'. This is true within broad limits, and perhaps the distinguishing feature of these mss. is that they include a section which is headed 'Sedra d'arzanayith' at the beginning of what we may call the 'Ordinary' of the Liturgy, whereas this feature is seldom if ever found in the older mss, nor in the Chaldean and Malabar mss. The mss. sometimes indicate that they are following the use of the Daira 'Ellaita, the Upper Monastery, that is, the Monastery of Mar Abraham and Mar Gabrial, near Mosul. Within this wide category, however, the mss. tend to fall into smaller groups, and rarely if ever does one find a ms. standing completely on its own. It should be noted that the greater number of variants tend to occur in the pre-anaphoral part of the rite. Thus Berlin 38 contains a large number of alternative prayers, some of which occur also in the British Museum's ms. Add. 7181, and in BN Paris.Syr.283. Berlin 41 is a late ms., but was copied from a much earlier Ritual, and has a text very similar to that of Mardin 19.[4]

Although the Franciscans had been at work in the area earlier, it was not until the middle of the sixteenth century that relations began to be established between part of the Nestorian Church and the See of Rome. By the end of the fifteenth century the Nestorian patriachate had become an hereditary office, passing from uncle to nephew or cousin with little regard being paid to the suitability of the person chosen. In 1551 this hereditary principle was challenged, when on the death of Sem'un bar Mama, the election of his nephew Sem'un Denha was disputed, and a group of bishops and heads of noble families elected John Sulaqa, a monk of the Rabban Hormidz monastery, as a rival

---

[1] There are Commentaries by Narsai, Gabriel Qatraya, Abraham bar Lipheh (merely an abbreviati on of Qatraya), the ninth century Pseudo-George of Arbel, and Johannan bar Zo'bi (based on Qatraya but with some interesting changes).

[2] BM. Add. 7181, dated 1881 A.G.=1570 A.D.

[3] Berlin 38 is dated 1496, and Macomber assigns Mardin 19, Cambr. Add 2046B and Diarbekir 48 to the fifteenth century. Rouen 21 he ascribes to the sixteenth century, but it could well be late fifteenth century.

Nestorian mss. can in many cases be accurately dated because of the custom of including a colophon, not always at the end, in which the scribe gives details of the place of writing, the date of its composition, and his name. The date is usually given in 'the year of the Greeks', and a rough rule is to subtract 311. Thus 1807 A.G. =1496 A.D.

[4] The list could be indefinitely extended. Thus Vat. Syr. 42 and Vat. Syr. 303 are very similar, and contain some interesting variants. From a partial transcript of the McHardy Ritual which I have seen, I would be inclined to think that its text is very similar to that of Alqosh 70.

patriarch. Thinking to strengthen his position, John Sulaqa applied to the Pope for recognition, and was sent by the Franciscans first to Jerusalem, and then to Rome, where, after submitting an acceptable statement of faith, he was ordained patriarch by Pope Julius III. However, on his return to Mesopotamia he was arrested and flung into prison by the Pasha of Diarbekir, and shortly afterwards murdered, almost certainly at the instigation of his rival. His successor, 'Abdisho', secured papal recognition in 1567.

Over two hundred years were to elapse, however, before the Chaldeans, as they were called, were provided with an official liturgy. For a time it continued to employ 'Nestorian' texts, presumably purged of 'errors', and this no doubt is why some of the mss. that have come down to us have had names like Nestorius and Narsai erased from the text. The question of an official text was raised towards the middle of the 18th century, but it was only after protracted discussions that the first printed edition of the Chaldean Missal appeared in 1767, printed at Rome, and published by decree of the Congregation de Propaganda Fide. However, a form of the rite had obviously been accepted more than half a century earlier, and a number of mss. of this rite, all showing more or less the same text, has come down to us. According to Dr. Macomber's list the earliest is Vat. Syr. 491, which is dated 1691. Cambr. Oo.1.15, written by the Metropolitan Simeon of Amida is dated 1691. At some stage in its history this ms. was taken from Rome, where it was written, to India, since it is part of the Buchanan Collection.[1] Quite a few Chaldean mss. were produced at the end of the 17th and beginning of the 18th centuries. In addition to those listed by Macomber, Bibliotheque Nationale, Paris Syr. 93, 95, 96 and 98 belong to this group. Some of these, it should be noted, were produced for the use of western scholars interested in the Chaldean rite rather than for use in church.[2] Another Chaldean text is to be found in Ouseley 267 in the Bodleian Library, Oxford, a bi-lingual ms. with a Syriac text of the Chaldean Liturgy and a Latin translation of the Malabar rite as revised by the Synod of Diamper, arranged in parallel columns.

What Dr. Macomber calls the 'Malabar tradition' is represented by only two mss. in his list; there are however a number of other mss. of this tradition.[3] There is no reason to suppose that the tradition which they represent is of any great antiquity, or that it is an ancient version of the Persian or Nestorian rite.

To understand the emergence of the rite in South India, it is necessary to study a little of its historical background. When the Portuguese arrived in India at the end of the fifteenth century, they found a church established since the sixth century, which obtained its bishops from Persia. It would seem that towards the end of the fifteenth century the Christians in Malabar had been without bishops for some time, for an embassy was sent to the Patriarch asking that bishops should be sent to India. F. C. Burkitt suggested that when, in response to that request, bishops arrived in India, they brought with them the service books which they used in Persia, and it was the rites as contained in these that the Portuguese found in use when they entered into relations with the Malabar Christians.[4]

---

[1] This collection is made up of a number of mss. collected by the Reverend George Buchanan while he was in India, and is now in the University Library, Cambridge.

[2] Thus Syr. 93 contains a version of the Chaldean Liturgy, beautifully written by a scribe named Basil, and a translation into Latin in all probability by the Abbe Deslandie for the great Oratorian scholar Pierre LeBrun. Syr. 97 is in the hand of Eusebuss Renaudot.

[3] Among them may be mentioned Bibliotheque Nationale Paris Syr. 89 (1689) 90 (1698), 91 and 92 (18th cen.); Vat. Syr. 290 (prior to 1751); Leiden Or. 1215 (Prior to 1720).

[4] F. C. Burkitt, 'The Old Malabar Liturgy'.

ADDAI AND MARI—THE ANAPHORA OF THE APOSTLES

Relations between the Malabar Christians and the Portuguese were initially very friendly, but soon the Portuguese began to discover 'errors' in the Indians' beliefs and practices. Eventually the Portuguese assumed control of the Malabar Church, an event which was made easier by the Chaldean succession. It was 'Abdisho', the successor of John Sulaqa who despatched Joseph Sulaqa, John's brother, to India as Metropolitan, with two Dominican friars as advisors. Though Mar Joseph was by no means inimical to Rome, and had even learned to celebrate the Latin Mass, he was always suspected by the Portuguese, and was three times sent to Europe charged with heresy. The third time he died at Rome (1568), and the books he had with him passed into the Vatican Library.

Among these books was Vat. Syr. 66, which contains a copy of the Liturgy of the Apostles, almost certainly written by Mar Joseph himself. Immediately before the liturgy, on a separate page, is a narrative of institution together with an indication that it is to be placed at the conclusion of the anaphora. De Gouvea tells us that the narrative of institution was introduced into the Malabar rite by a certain archbishop more learned than the rest, and it would seem that Mar Joseph was this particular archbishop.

The Synod of Diamper, convened by Alexis de Menezes, Archbishop of Goa, in 1599 produced a series of amendments to the liturgy as it was then celebrated, but apart from the inclusion of the institution narrative, it differed little from the contemporary Nestorian rite. There is no evidence, however, that the amended rite of the Synod enjoyed either popularity or use. One may suspect that it was not 'latinized' enough for the Portuguese.[1] The printed missal which appeared in 1774 presented a very different text. The author of this version which was officially adopted was almost certainly Francis Roz, sj., Bishop of Angamale, and it dates from about 1606. The mss. of this rite that have survived are later than this, but the text they contain is very similar to that adopted in the 1774 printed missal.[2]

One other ms. deserves mention: Bibliotheque Nationale Syr. 88. Its title reads 'Liturgy of the Holy Apostles accordingto the rite of the Chaldean Syrians', but its contents are very different. It is written in Syriac, Carshuni (Arabic in Syriac characters) and Arabic. It contains parts of the Liturgy of the Apostles, with some of the Qanonas from the other two Nestorian anaphoras, but the central part of the Eucharistic prayer is taken from Maronite *Sharar*. This strange mixture is followed by the Anaphora of the Twelve Apostles (also Maronite) and a Diaconal which is not Chaldean. There is no indication of date, or the scribe's name, but it would appear to be eighteenth century, and was presumably written for some orientalist (or reconstructor of original texts?) in the West.

[1] See J. Vellian, Encounter of the West with the East in Malabar, in *The Romanization Tendency*, The Syrian Churches Series, Vol. 8, Kottayam 1975, pp.70-84.

[2] E. R. Hambye, 'Un manuscrit oublie de la Liturgie Syro-Malabare Latinizee', in *Memorial Mgr. Gabriel Khouri-Sarkis*, Louvain 1969, describes a ms. in the Ajuda Library, Lisbon, dated 1604, which contains a version of the Liturgy which must be one of the earliest mss. of the Malabar rite.

Three articles by C. Moussess in *Le Proche-Orient Chretien* 1 (1951) 2 (1952) and 4 (1954) give useful information on the Nestorian, Chaldean and Malabar forms of the Liturgy.

BIBLIOGRAPHY
English Language

F. C. Burkitt, 'The Old Malabar Liturgy' in *JTS* 29 (1928), pp.155-157.

R. H. Connolly, E. Bishop, 'The Work of Menezes on the Malabar Liturgy' in *JTS* 15 (1914) pp.396-425; 569-589.

E. Cutrone, 'The Anaphora of the Apostles: Implications of the Mar Esa'ya Text' in *TS* 43 (1973), pp.624-642.

R. J. Galvin, 'Addai and Mari revisited: The state of the Question' in *EL* 87 (1973) pp.383-414.

Bayard H. Jones, 'The History of the Nestorian Liturgies' in *ATR* 46 (1964) pp.155-176.